D1234531

"Sensible Sex"

A Guide for Newlyweds

"Sensible Sex"

A GUIDE FOR NEWLYWEDS

LINDSAY R. CURTIS, M.D.

Also published under title of
"And They Shall Be One Flesh"

Publishers Press
1881 West North Temple
Salt Lake City, Utah 84116

Copyright © 1968 by
Lindsay R. Curtis, M.D.
3107 Polk
Ogden, Utah 84403

HQ
31
.C8

Foreword

If you are one of those individuals who feels that sex is dirty, if you believe that sex is undiscussible, if you think that sex is unimportant, DON'T READ THIS BOOK! Forget it. It will be a waste of your time.

On the other hand, if you feel that sex is God-given, vital to a successful marriage, if you are convinced that sex can be and should be that marvelous part of life that welds inseparable bonds between a man and his wife, then this book is for you. If you also feel that sex is something that requires love, tenderness, compassion and skill, then this booklet will help you and your wife to greater love, understanding . . . and unity.

Hopefully you will achieve these noble goals.

The Author

ALMA COLLEGE
MONTEITH LIBRARY
ALMA, MICHIGAN

Acknowledgments

Grateful appreciation is expressed to my colleagues, Dr. Thomas M. Feeny and Dr. William R. Egbert for their comments and suggestions and to Mrs. Marilyn B. Hansen for her meticulous typing of the script.

Contents

CHAPTER 1

The Solution to the "In-Law" Problem

No sooner had God given Eve to Adam as a wife than He said: "Therefore shall a man *leave* his father and his mother, and shall cleave unto his wife: AND THEY SHALL BE ONE FLESH." Genesis 2:24. It would seem that God in His wisdom anticipated many problems that would eternally nag the human race, not the least of which would be "in-law" relationships.

We find an important clue in that particular verse. What it says is not that we should love our parents less, but that when we take a husband or wife we must love them *MORE* than anyone else. And if this advice is meticulously followed, we have the beginning of a successful marriage relationship.

This is not to say that a young couple does not need advice and counsel. Quite the opposite. Sage counsel of the proper type may prevent them from foundering in countless costly mistakes.

However, in-laws would do well to quietly assume the attitude: "You call us, we'll not bother you!" To effectively play this role requires tacit tongue-biting and an occasional *private* I-knew-it-would-happen sigh as they make multiple mistakes. But if parents can carry off this corner-of-the-eye observation in subtle silence, their relationship with the newly-marrieds will be unimpaired.

Even if young people make mistakes, they do not want to be reminded nor have such brought to their attention. They usually know only too well that they have made a gross error and want to forget it as soon as possible.

After observing the adverse effect upon the physical side of marriage that living-in with and/or renting-from in-laws has upon a young couple, I feel inclined to accept the literality of the scripture in Genesis 2:24: "Therefore shall a man LEAVE his father and mother". . . . and to paraphrase, "move away into his own apartment with his wife" where they will have privacy and the chance to make their own decisions.

Many a bride has confided complete failure in their sexual life because of the lack of privacy while living with parents, or even in the immediate vicinity of their in-laws. In this case, two make for a romantic canoe cruise, but any extra passengers may sink the boat.

"Now far be it from me to try to run your lives for you, but . . ." too often is merely a prelude allowing the well-meaning advice-giver license to run the young couple's life for them. The ultimate result is that they "ruin," rather than "run" such lives.

Ten

As for the young couple, you can simply solve the in-law problem by assuming the attitude of respectful attention while parents proffer their well-intended advice, then "cleave unto your wives or husbands" while you deliberate and come to a united decision . . . of your own.

And parents, don't be offended if young people don't take your advice. Feel flattered if they ask you for advice, but be prepared to have them do exactly the opposite. In fact, *permit* them to do exactly the opposite to what you have advised them.

CHAPTER 2

Communication? No Comment!

In spite of the fact that man has the most intricate means of communication imaginable, he can still learn much from animals. Whether it be hogs noisily crowding each other at the feeding trough, or the undetectable message between a male and female moth a half mile apart, there is unquestioned communication.

Regardless of whether it be chickens cackling and cluck-ing or the silent sonar transmission between bats or porpoises, they seem to have no problem getting their message through to each other. Only the human being, who enjoys the most intricate equipment of all, has this trouble. Only humans can sit and suffer and sulk in silence, afraid to offer the first word of apology to each other, or to show even the slightest sign of sincere, self-accusing compromise.

There are very few problems in marriage that cannot be solved by talking them out. Yet for some reason or other, the conference table of marriage finds its chairs unoccupied, its participants unable to bargain with each other, its contestants unwilling to seek common ground.

As far as man and wife are concerned, there could never be a more important conference held. And if children are involved, there could never be more at stake than their happiness. How easy it is to take a small step on the bridge of compromise across a tiny streamlet of water that separates a man and his wife, instead of waiting until that same streamlet grows into a raging torrent of unsettled and unresolved problems, a torrent of water raging 'neath the bridge of indifference.

Long before a lawyer is required for arbitration in the monstrous problems of marriage, the tiny misunderstandings could have been resolved by the couple themselves. And an extremely fair and unbiased arbiter could have been found as close as to shut their eyes. How simple it is to say: "Help us Lord to understand each other and talk our differences over . . . and out. May we find in their place many likenesses and great love."

It's a rare couple that precedes their connubial conference with a shared, soulful supplication to their God, that doesn't find complete mutual understanding. Kneeling together at bedside, arm in arm, there comes no closer communication than this sacred moment with their Maker.

If our courts were to simply lock many of the divorce-demanding duos in a room and tell them to stay until they compromised their problems and could come out arm in arm, they would undoubtedly do it. Perhaps not without a few blows and scars of the scuffle, but the quarreling couple might find their differences dissolving into doit.

In short, find out before marriage if you can talk things OUT before you talk each other IN-to saying "I do."

CHAPTER 3

A Sin Greater Than Ingratitude

By all the usual standards Sid is successful. He is Branch Manager for his firm and this undoubtedly is only the beginning of the upward ladder as far as his ultimate potential is concerned. His wife Marti enjoys a spacious home in the better part of town, a home that is graced with tasteful but expensive accoutrements. Sid commands the respect of his employees and is president of his service club.

His family consists of three dutiful, intelligent children who almost worship their father. Sickness to this family is practically unknown.

What more then, could Sid possibly ask from life?

Let Sid tell his own story. "Doctor, I love Marti very deeply. I'm sure you know that. I feel safe in saying that she loves me also. Yet I can't go on living with her the way we are and still maintain any dignity or self respect.

"I don't believe that I am oversexed, nor overdemanding, but a man just doesn't live with a beautiful wife whom he adores, and have to treat her like a sister. I don't mean that Marti *refuses* to have intercourse, but she has a way of making me feel that she tolerates it *only for me,* and this she does begrudgingly. I feel like a beggar instead of a lover.

"At night she goes to bed early and feigns sound asleep when I come to bed. Or else she refuses to come to bed with me on the ruse that she wants to watch a certain television show. Or she is too tired, or has a headache . . . or something else. And all of this after she has chased around all day doing things that she seemed to have plenty of energy for.

"In short, Doctor, what she is saying in her heart is this: 'If you want it, you'll pay for it.' I have to beg and plead for affection. It's so humiliating that I'm not sure I can take it any longer."

Marti, on the other hand, was in the office this week with a different side of the story.

"Sid just wants me for someone to sleep with. That's all he thinks of. Why doesn't he get those childish things out of his mind?"

The truth proved to be somewhere in between. But the real problem could be summed up in one word that nurtures many different facets. That word is "rejection." Rejection begets humiliation. Humiliation espouses resentment. Resentment builds into hatred . . . and the marriage "built on love" now finds the same two people working *against* each other. .

Eighteen

How did Sid and Marti actually come to reject each other?

Sid, it seems, failed to notice and appreciate the little things Marti did for him, like a special dish for dinner, flowers on the table, an extra effort to clean up the mess after the children, to look nice when he got home. The many spats between the children that Marti settled *before* "Dad got home" may have been unknown to Sid, but if he had just told Marti a little oftener how much he loved her. If he had just noticed a few of the little things and told her how proud he was of her. Such thoughtfulness would have revived her waning morale.

But after being "rejected" repeatedly herself, Marti began subconsciously to "get even" with Sid in the way she knew would hurt his own morale and confidence the most. By denying him intercourse, Marti destroyed the self-esteem that a man should have, the knowledge that his wife *wants* him and needs him.

Sid, on the other hand, because he was hurt, complimented Marti even less, (even though he subconsciously knew that she NEEDED this extra attention), in order to get back at her for rejecting him. Thus they went on their merry and very unhappy way, rejecting each other more and more and doing everything they could to make each other unhappy.

After a rather frank talk, I asked them how they would like to put as much effort into making their marriage work as they were doing to make it fail. Naturally it has succeeded.

Nineteen

Sid didn't really want, need or expect intercourse as often as he requested it. But a child wants candy badly only if he can't have it. If it were all around him for the taking he would soon turn his back on it. On the other hand, Marti also was a normal woman with normal desires which were not being fulfilled.

Men, and women too, crave that which they cannot have. A wise woman not only realizes this, but she also senses that there is no heartbreak quite equal to the heartbreak of humiliation. This she will spare her husband at all costs. And he will spare her the same.

There is an unspoken language in a successful marriage that tells a wife when her husband desires her and she, if she is wise, beats him to the punch by preparing herself. The husband's ego is sustained, he is convinced his wife still loves and can't do without him, and she secretly smiles to herself as he lays the world at the feet of the woman he worships.

Twenty

CHAPTER 4

"... And They Were Not Ashamed : :."

"My wife doesn't undress to go to bed. She merely changes clothes." So complained one husband to me concerning his spouse.

"My husband insists that we sleep in the nude all the time. And he isn't as careful about modesty around the children as he should be." Such was the objection from a 31-year-old woman who continued: "I'm no prude, but this is carrying things too far. Isn't there any place for modesty after marriage?"

Yes, there is a place for modesty after marriage and even in the bedroom. Although the two cases above may represent the two extremes, there are many situations in between these two that cause some problems.

One of the best investments after purchasing a double bed is to buy an electric blanket with dual controls so that husband and wife may share the same bed without one making the other uncomfortable. This might also solve the problem of the first case mentioned so that she would not have to wear so many clothes to bed . . . or does she do it for another reason?

Naturally when two young people are first married there is a certain amount of curiosity to be satisfied. This is understandable and perhaps desirable on the part of both, but each should respect the privacy of the other. Especially when it comes to certain physiologic functions, each will desire complete privacy from the other and from children.

However, there is a time during which man and wife belong to each other. It is difficult for them to be "as one flesh" if they have clothing between them. Within the sacred bonds of marriage this is neither sensual nor is it evil or nasty. This is the *one time* during which God-given emotions and feelings should be given full and complete expression. There should be absolutely no thought that the act is wicked, forbidden, frowned upon, or that it is giving vent to abnormal or beastly tendencies.

At no time do a man and wife feel closer to each other spiritually as well as physically than during this strictly private and confidential event. It is interesting that Adam and Eve set us the pattern, a pattern that was later recorded by Moses in Genesis 2:25, as follows: "And they were both naked and *they were not ashamed!*"

A wise wife clothes herself just enough to leave something to her husband's imagination, for an imagination can picture her even more beautiful than she really is. An appropriate sheer negligee enhances the beauty of the nude body like a soft screen improves a photographer's portrait.

Needless to say, both husband and wife should be modest around their children. Although there are some who feel they should unabashedly parade in front of their children in any or no attire in order to teach them "about life," experience does not seem to be in their favor. There is an appropriate time and place and atmosphere in which to teach young people about life and in most cases this is best done in the home and by parents. But it is not done by ignoring social customs and mores. There is no excuse for discarding all semblance of refinement and culture. While men are usually the worst offenders in this respect, when a woman becomes coarse, she is to most people, disgusting.

If a husband wishes to cuddle up to his wife and to lovingly "feel" her presence beside him, a wife should feel flattered. However, this does not have to be in the constant nude. That which becomes commonplace, often becomes uninteresting.

Twenty-three

CHAPTER 5

Preparation Pays

It was a tired, harrassed, disappointed and hurt voice on the other end of the telephone that sobbed out these words: "Doctor, can I come to see you right away? It's really urgent. In fact, I'm nearly out of my mind." Betty was married two days ago and left for an extended and long planned-for honeymoon, which had terminated abruptly so that she could return home to see her doctor.

And poor, frustrated and bewildered Bob was at her side, hangdoggedly solicitous and obviously feeling guilty. Their two nights together had turned out to be anything but the grand and glorious bed of clouds they had thought it was going to be. Much to the consternation, embarrassment, frustration and total disappointment of Bob and to the terrified, hurt and benumbed Betty, they had been completely unable to consummate their marriage.

Betty decided she had made a mistake to marry at all. She had no idea a man looked like THAT! And it was so painful! Bob, on the other hand, found that in spite of tenderness and gentleness on his part, she simply would not cooperate.

Now then, how might this unfortunate beginning have been avoided? What had they failed to do? Wherein had this intelligent young couple gone wrong?

Not only was Betty a virgin, but she had never had a pelvic examination in her life. Her mother had told her only one thing, that sex was nasty and that she should keep hands away from "her lady parts." She had also been told that "nice young girls" don't use internal tampons for menstrual protection because they are harmful.

The truth is that nice young girls can be cleaner and more santiary if they WILL use internal tampons. Such protection will allow them greater freedom with all activities, including sports, and cultivate the healthy attitude that this is not a "sick time" at all. Women may carry on just as they normally do with unrestricted activities.

In addition, internal tampons teach women about their anatomy and help to prepare them for marriage. By stretching the hymen (maidenhead), tampons prepare the way, so to speak enabling the doctor, on premarital check-up to perform a more adequate examination. He then, under local anesthesia, can stretch the hymen further if necessary to avoid the painful and traumatic "first night" of an otherwise heavenly honeymoon.

Does this stretching of the hymen rob a girl of her virginity? By definition, a virgin is a woman who has not had sexual intercourse. Stretched hymen or not, the girl's virginity is preserved.

Let's talk about another question. Should the engaged couple read a good book on the sexual side of marriage together to help prepare them? Although this is a choice that each couple must make, I do have an opinion.

One of the reasons a girl and boy decide they are meant for each other is the fact that they can talk together. This means that they can talk about anything and they usually do. However, when it comes to studying the intimate details of married life together . . . before they are married, . . . this they sometimes find difficult to do. And those who do so sometimes find it takes something away from the actual experience of being married. After all, this experience comes to them only once in their lifetime (hopefully). If they have explored all of the possibilities beforehand, even vicariously through a book, much of the thrill may be gone.

An important part of a honeymoon is the opportunity of the bride and groom to LEARN TOGETHER. In fact, this is the purpose of the honeymoon, to allow the couple to go away into complete seclusion and privacy while they do LEARN TOGETHER. If they have tried to learn this beforehand, even by reading about it, some of the thrill may be lost.

Ideally a couple should have a BRIEF, very much to the point handbook on the sexual side of marriage to take with them on their honeymoon. This they can read together as they learn. And may I repeat again because of its importance, the bride-to-be should have a complete examination including a pelvic examination and preparation of the hymen before marriage.

As far as counseling on the social side of marriage, this is often best done by a spiritual adviser. *He* can best encourage them in the necessity for unselfishness, consideration and kindness, etc.

CHAPTER 6

... And Vice Versa

Secretly every man thinks that he is God's gift to women. Too often during the dating stage he has been treated this way. It is only natural then that he takes the "love, honor, and obey" very literally and even points an "isn't this what I've been trying to tell you" finger at the passage, "wives submit to your husbands." (Eph. 5:22)

Understandably a man thinks that just because he thrilled his wife with every kiss before they were married that, with no further concern, he will continue to do so AFTER they are married. Such might continue, but only if he works hard at it.

Before marriage a man is on his best behavior. He is out to impress his girl friend. He is congenial, generous, clever (if he can be), conversational, tender, and almost over-solicitous. Every gesture is so maneuvered that it will impress her favorably and prepare her to *be* thrilled when he kisses her goodnight.

Small wonder then, that when he does finally get around to that much awaited, much planned-for goodnight kiss, that she is ecstatic, floating several inches off the ground, convinced that she is being courted by an impeccable lover, a gallant knight with flawless manners, a gentleman to the core, an unselfish, sacrificing future husband who will always keep her on a pedestal and place her wants and her desires far above his own.

Who could possibly refuse to love, honor, obey and submit to such a mate for the rest of her life?

Some men have managed to preserve such an unearthly image, but none that I know personally. However, there are many men working at it and these are the husbands whose wives still love, honor, cherish and are thrilled not only to submit themselves, but these wives cleverly and subtly maneuver their husbands into submitting also.

Husbands, just because your sweetheart has two rings on her finger does not mean that you cease to open the car door for her, or that you no longer find ways to please and surprise her. It doesn't mean that you stop complimenting her on her appearance, her cooking, her sewing, yes, even her cleaning. In fact, if you're smart you help her with the latter.

When a man has a wife who becomes unromantic, he should first look at himself. Here are just a few comments by wives who have lost the glamour of romance in their marriage.

"Why can't he shave and use a little cologne first?"

"He always takes a shower before he goes to work in the morning. Why not before he goes to bed?"

Thirty

"He finds fault with me all evening, then expects me to go to bed and be romantic."

"He sits and reads the paper or watches television while I do all the dishes and fight my way through putting the children to bed all by myself, then he wonders why I am too tired and exasperated to respond to him."

"He is so stingy with money that he takes away all my self-respect. If he would just give me a small allowance that is MINE to do with as I please and for which I don't have to answer and explain to him. I might even spend it on something nice *for him*. But when he approaches me now, I find only resentment building up."

"He seems to find money for golf, bowling, fishing and for guns, but he never has enough for just a few things to fix up the house. I think I'll go to work so I'll have MY money to do with what I want. And then he wonders why I can't get thrilled with him in bed."

Although these barbs are directed at the husband, there are counterparts, although less often, in certain wives. The commonest complaint in a wife is overweight. Native Hawaiians want their wives to be fat and our hats are off to them if this is their custom. But here on the mainland, custom and social preferences demand that a woman avoid those ugly extra pounds. It is possible for EVERYONE, without exception, to lose weight and to maintain a given weight. All it takes is the proper motivation.

Thirty-one

If a woman (or a man, for that matter) wants to be thin more than she wants to be fat, she can lose weight. If she is motivated more in the other direction, i.e. enjoys eating more than being thin, then she will not lose weight.

Cleanliness is occasionally a complaint. A woman should learn the art of marital hygiene, including douching prior to intercourse when she has an unpleasant discharge. Curlers may have become a necessary part of modern life, yet some women find ways to accomplish this when their husbands are away, or change their hair style so they won't need them.

Tobacco breath along with halitosis can be challenged by mouth washes and sprays, at least prior to going to bed.

In conclusion, may we suggest that if husbands and wives seek only to *please* each other, there will be no need for either one to submit.

CHAPTER 7

"Rejoice with the Wife of Thy Youth"

Proverbs 5:18

Jill was just 26, pert and pretty, sparkling jet-black eyes flashing a fascinating contrast to her ivory-white teeth. Unfortunately her chin quivered as her lips fumbled nervously for words to express her awkward situation.

"I love Jed with all my heart and I'm sure he loves me just as much. Perhaps that's the trouble. It might be easier if we didn't love each other so much. But we just can't go on like this. We have one child and we are not ready for another one yet. So what do we do in the meantime?"

"Well if that is the only problem," I started to say.

"You don't understand. Jed is very religious and determined to live as he should. When we went for religious counseling before we were married our religious counselor told us that we were never to have relations unless we wanted a baby. In fact, he said there was to be no thought of what he called "sensuality" in our relationship. Our marriage has been one great nightmare of frustration.

That, to me, seemed to be the understatement of all time. Either they had misunderstood the religious counselor, or the religious counselor had lost a tooth out of his mental gears. For no one in his right mind could possibly counsel a young couple in this way. However, it does bring up an interesting facet of marriage. Is it normal, natural and moral to *enjoy* intercourse?

I doubt that the Lord would have made it so, had He not in His great wisdom intended it to be that way. In this manner he made sure that the race would propagate itself.

Should a couple enjoy intercourse even when they don't think it will result in a pregnancy? It scarcely seems necessary to discuss yet there are some religious advisers who equate anything sexual with evil. Sex itself is not evil. Sex is God-given and God-intended for marriage and a marriage without proper sex adjustment usually is far from what the Lord intended that union to be.

"Rejoice with the wife of thy youth" (Proverbs 5:18) is what the Bible tells us and there is nothing to indicate that the sexual relationship within the confines of marriage should be anything but a pleasurable, beautifully serene experience in which a man and woman reaffirm their love for each other.

To relegate sexual intercourse to the single purpose of procreation is to equate it with the same act in lower animals, since this is its only purpose in other than human beings. Surely the Lord did not give us the intelligence as well as the strong sexual emotions merely to taunt us. Naturally He expects us to use good judgment and to control these instincts, but He also gave them to us knowing that they could weld a bond beween husband and wife that would give stability to the home.

To answer the question, "Is it wrong to enjoy intercourse?" Absolutely not, and if it is *not* enjoyable within the bounds of marriage, then the couple needs some help and counseling.

CHAPTER 8

Setting the Stage

Our behavior is based to a great extent upon our attitudes. Unfortunately a man and a woman enter into marriage with widely differing concepts of what marriage is and should be. Usually both are completely wrong, especially in relation to sex and the part it should play in marriage.

Sex in marriage is proper, it is decent, it is necessary. When successful it is divine. Sex in marriage provides the oil that makes the machinery of family life run smoothly. It is the magic cement that holds a marriage together when other problems threaten to tear it apart. Sex is the most intimate, private and sacred facet of marriage and one of the few that is never shared with anyone else, including the children.

The responsibility for the success of this side of marriage is bilateral, placing equally this task upon each partner, with a promise that each will receive from the relationship just about what he or she puts into it. If a man thinks only of himself, he will find a wife that eventually freezes up toward him and recognizes him for what he is, a selfish, self-centered animal. On the other hand, a wife who will not contribute of herself to the relationship soon finds her husband withdrawing the non-reciprocal projection of his affection. Such a wife shouldn't be too surprised to find her husband searching elsewhere for the affection she fails to give him.

Armed then with a healthy attitude toward sex in marriage, the co-directors of this production can set about to make it the finest production of their lives and one that will continue successful reruns as long as they live.

Any successful play begins with enthusiasm and optimism. But these must be sufficient to weather temporary failures or set-backs. The directors must have confidence that they have a combination that will ultimately be a smash hit.

In order to have a success, however, considerable thought, time and effort must be expended. Proper lighting, costuming, sometimes trial and error and certainly plenty of practice all are included in the list of essentials. Young people must not expect sex in marriage to come in the instant-success package. If there is sufficient love and tenderness and patience in each partner, ultimate mutual enjoyment will be the end result.

It is not uncommon for a bridegroom to fail completely in the sex act on the first night. When this happens he wonders what is wrong with himself. He forgets the excitement, the fatigue, the anxiety of the ordeal. But time and rest and patience correct all this.

Even more common is the failure of the bride to achieve any kind of climax or orgasm, not only the first night, but for some time after marriage. Unless she has been properly informed she may wonder what has happened to the feelings she had for her husband before they were married. She may think they are not suited to each other, or that she has married the wrong man. All this, of course, is untrue. Whereas in a man most of this response comes with no effort on his part, in a woman it must be cultivated. She must be educated to a proper response.

It is most important at a time like this that the husband be patient and tender and considerate of his wife. He must not force, nor hurry her. He must convince her of his love and his consideration for her as his life-long companion and sweetheart, not just as his bed partner. His patience at this crucial time may determine much of their future relationship.

If he must wait for a few nights until they become used to each other, he should sense this. If she has not been examined and prepared by a physician, he should encourage her to do so. Above all he must not hurt her. If the hymen is intact and is too rigid, he should take her to a physician to have this skilfully stretched under anesthesia.

A husband must remember that the transition from virginity and cautious chastity to the role of a willing wife may be extremely frightening to her. Only he can help her to make this transition smoothly and without emotional trauma.

CHAPTER 9

The Woman's Role

No joy approaches the mutually shared ecstasy of the culmination of a proper love embrace. This is God's intended method of making them "one flesh." Never do husband and wife blend more completely, never do they feel closer and more united than at this blessed moment.

However, this is achieved only when the wife also gives of herself completely, lending active and unrestrained response to her husband's embraces. This is the time for discarding natural reserves and timidity. This is the time when she should feel free to tell her husband how to caress her so that she may respond.

A wife should, in a subtle and almost imperceptible way, coach and train and direct her husband to help him become the ideal lover for HER. After all, if they are to spend a lifetime togther, they should begin by becoming adept at this very important part of their relationship as husband and wife.

Forty-one

Half the pleasure a man derives from intercourse is in thrilling his wife. If he fails to achieve this, he feels he has failed indeed. His ego is deflated and he is certain that he is not the man he thought he was.

A considerate husband will, of course ask his wife if she is enjoying intercourse and if there is anything he can do differently to help her to enjoy it. It is *her* responsibility to tell him this and to cautiously offer suggestions as to what might intensify her enjoyment.

It is not uncommon for a wife to fail to reach a climax sometime when they have intercourse, but this is not serious . . . if both husband and wife understand that this is not serious. A man's sexual need may be greater than his wife's, but she, in turn may occasionally enjoy just being held in his arms and knowing that she is loved, while he completes the act.

A wise wife may choose on occasion to feign complete response, knowing that this will heighten his satisfaction and merely lead him to love her that much more. In this case, she receives a certain amount of satisfaction just knowing that she is the one and only woman for him.

When she clutches him tightly to her, whether climaxing or not, he knows that he is being accepted, not rejected, and it is a mutual and shared love that is being given expression. Ultimately she receives in return manyfold the love and tolerance and understanding that she is giving her husband at this time.

However, a woman should normally respond in intercourse and if both she and her husband will work at it, she will probably find that she is capable of responding better and more completely than he does. How often we find a woman who reaches the first climax of her life only after many years of complacent tolerance for something she thought she was not meant to enjoy. And all it took for this change was a little instruction and effort by both of them.

After 25 years of married life one patient stopped in the office to see me just as she was on her way to a lawyer to obtain a divorce because of sexual maladjustment. After some instruction she discovered that she was normal after all and so was her husband. All they needed was a little change in technique. "And to think that we wasted 25 good years," was her only comment.

Although cautious not to offend him, a wife should never be hesitant to tell her husband what gives her the most pleasure. If certain positions are more satisfactory, if some movements aid her in achieving her orgasm she should tell him. If some of his caresses are distasteful or annoying, she may also tactfully let him know that some other caresses are more satisfying.

Some women prefer to have the clitoris titillated just before but not during the climax. Others cannot achieve satisfaction without constant titillation. Still others achieve the same result by lying on top of their husbands during the act. But the husband cannot be aware of these things unless his wife lets him know in one way or another.

Couples should not hesitate to experiment with different positions and different types of caresses during coitus. Only in this way can they determine what is best for THEM. There really are no rules to govern the intimacies between husband and wife. It is no one else's business. That which is mutually agreeable and pleasurable and contributes to the mutual satisfaction and enjoyment of the act is the only governing factor.

What is satisfactory for someone else may be repulsive to you. What you have found to be delightful for you, may not appeal to others. This is private. It is intimate. It is confidential and should be reserved for you and your husband.

Is it normal for a woman to actively participate in intercourse? Of course. Unfortunately some people have grown up in a culture that teaches intercourse is only to satisfy the beastly instincts of a man. Of course this is not so. The Lord did not intend it to be so. A woman is designed physiologically so that she can respond just as well or even more so than a man.

In the wooing prior to intercourse a woman should not only respond to her husband's kisses, embraces and caresses, but she should also actively participate in all of these herself. She should feel free to caress and fondle and do anything else that she knows is pleasurable to either one of them.

During intercourse it is not only proper but desirable for her to use the muscles of her vagina to enhance the pleasure of the act in both of them. No one wishes to sleep with a dead fish. A woman can learn to manipulate the muscles of her vagina so that it intensifies the feeling for both her and her husband. Nor should she stop these movements until her husband is completely finished with his ejaculation. This produces the maximum amount of sensation in both.

A husband appreciates a reciprocation of his advances. He interprets caresses by his wife as an indication of acceptance of him.

Is it abnormal for a woman to reach several orgasms per love-act? Definitely not. It is not only normal, but fairly common, although not mandatory. The ultimate goal should be for the husband to help his wife to achieve the pleasure, the enjoyment, the closeness, the unspoken love that such an act was meant to convey. Such a mutually enjoyable experience is on the highest spiritual plane. It is fulfillment of the God-given commandment.

No one would ask for more than this.

CHAPTER 10

The Man's Role

Only in extreme cases is a woman really frigid. Only rarely is a woman unable to respond to a man she loves, if he is skilled enough to prepare her for the act and then follow through in the way he should.

Not only are few women frigid, but most women, if properly inspired, will desire intercourse almost as often as men and will respond just as completely. While it is true that some few women are more passionate than men, and some others respond with greater passion even to being kissed, the majority of women must be wooed before they respond at all.

And many women who are frigid, withdrawn, nervous, irritable and hate their husbands, have been brought to this condition by an inconsiderate, inept husband who completely bungled the sex-act and conditioned them to think that all men are of this type.

A woman is much like a beautiful musical instrument. She must first be warmed up and put in tune, then delicately and masterfully handled in order to bring out harmonious and inspiring music. If handled clumsily, harshly, or indelicately, the resultant sounds are offensive and unpleasant.

We don't have to be master-musicians, however, to learn how to bring out the best in our wives. A good musician takes good care of his instrument even when it is not in use. He cherishes and values it for its true worth. Just as with the musical instrument, a man should cherish his wife and treat her *always* as a sweetheart, not just when he anticipates a concert.

Even if a man has a sex-drive geared to a harem, he will find a responsive wife if he truly loves, respects, and honors her in EVERYTHING ELSE. Never was anything more valid than "bread cast upon the waters" when it comes to matters of sex.

Admittedly there are cases of outright selfishness either in the man with his demands, or in a woman who makes her husband pay and pay dearly for any response she gives him, just as though she were a prostitute instead of a wife. But these are the exception and not the rule.

If husbands will constantly keep in mind: "What can I do to please my wife most? How does she feel about this? She must come first. If she enjoys it, then I will be happy."

Such unselfish reasoning will usually result in a completely satisfying experience for both, for when the wife responds, the response in the husband is enhanced manyfold.

Never should a husband plunge headlong into the act of intercourse when his wife is unprepared, unaroused, or unwilling. Preparation for the next intercourse should have begun all over again following the last act. This includes tenderness of the wife's feelings, helpfulness with the children, overlooking her faults and magnifying her accomplishments.

One can scarcely blame a woman for being unresponsive if the only time she hears a kind word is when her husband wants intercourse. A stage properly set, is the first step toward a smash hit. Treat your wife like a queen and she will respond as if you were a king.

God made man (or most men) to be aggressive sexually. Likewise most men are turned on sexually at the drop of a woman's eyelash. But a woman (or most women) must be wooed from the first word to the final embrace. A wise husband treats his wife as his perennial sweetheart.

The poorest man on earth is still loaded with gifts that will please a woman if he chooses to give them. If a pauper is full of praise for his wife she will love and treasure this reassurance far above the most expensive and lavish gift he could find. Words, tenderly put together, provide the combination that unlocks the innermost chambers of a woman's heart.

Next in importance are gestures of tenderness that clearly shows that a husband is more interested in his wife's joy than in his own. A woman is so designed that she responds readily to tender caressing of her entire body more than she does to direct stimulation of her genitals. Many a husband thinks his wife is cold, when in reality he has not taken the time nor expended the effort to skilfully and tenderly warm her up.

A woman wants to be kissed and loved and talked to. To a man the climax may be the only crucial part of the relationship and he is eager to get to the point right now. But to a woman, the foreplay and the afterglow, the feeling of being wanted and loved may be equal to or even greater in importance than the actual climax.

To a husband ,the only important thing in the meal is the steak. But to his wife, the side dishes really make the meal.

CHAPTER 11

The Sex Act

The sex act has a different meaning for the man and for the woman. A man too often feels that the sex act begins with the insertion of the penis and ends when it is withdrawn. But for the woman the act consists of three parts:

1. The foreplay or preparation

2. *The sex act proper*

3. The afterplay

Although we don't wish to detract any from the sex act proper, to a woman the foreplay and afterplay may be just as important and perhaps even more enjoyable, for in these she finds the tenderness and gentleness that are so meaningful to her.

Successful intercourse occurs when both partners are completely satisfied. In such a relationship, each partner must feel free and uninhibited. Each must feel free to tell the other of his or her feelings and thereby to guide his partner to the most satisfying response.

This is the one time in life when modesty is out of place, for husband and wife are to be 'as one flesh." Caresses should be spontaneous, fleeting, and gentle. In a truly successful relationship there is no passive partner. Many marriages suffer because the wife "expects" a quiet, otherwise retiring husband to be the complete aggressor. Perhaps in every day life it is she who is the aggressive one. It may be impossible for him to step out of character and become aggressive. And any attempt by his wife to force him to do this is hazardous and leads to misunderstandings.

Intercourse is just what it says, a relationship *between* two people, not some act imposed by one upon another. Most young husbands are eager and willing to *initiate* love play, but they have a right to expect their bride to *respond* to such advances enthusiastically. Nothing will cool and remove the bright lustre of young married love quicker than a cool, silent, sullen, negative attitude toward the bridegroom's advances.

Either from misdirected or maladjusted parents or from well-meaning but misinformed friends the bride may have heard that it is uncommon for a woman to achieve an orgasm or climax. Nothing could be farther from the truth. It is not only uncommon for a woman *not* to have an orgasm, but it is rare to find a woman who is incapable of an orgasm when she is properly stimulated.

The fault too often lies in either fear or faulty technique. Most cases of so-called frigidity that I have seen began with poor preparation for marriage, a frustrating and fearful honeymoon, followed by a prolonged period of disappointing, one-sided blundering and boredom in marriage that conditioned the woman almost beyond help.

After a few weeks of adjustment, if a new bride finds she is unable to experience an orgasm, she, along with her husband should seek medical help and advice.

One final word as to what is normal and what is not in marriage. As I mentioned earlier, there are few rules to go by in this very private relationship between a man and his wife, but one rule holds supreme: whatever is done must be acceptable to both partners. Nothing that appeals to the imagination of either partner and is not repulsive or unacceptable to the other should be considered abnormal.

It is well to remember that nearly all variations attempted by the average couple have been tried before . . . by nearly every other couple. This applies to varities of positions, types of caresses, and any other innovations.

It is man's nature to be adventurous. He may *think* he has discovered something new and different. He hasn't. But at least he provides some variation and interest to a vital part of marriage that otherwise could become trite, stereotyped and even boringly routine.

The bride, on the other hand, must overcome modesty and tradition if she is to be rewarded by her husband's love, appreciation and in most cases, her own increased pleasure. She must not view her husband's adventurousness as nasty, vulgar, or abnormal, unless the unusual is insisted upon as the standard.

Fifty-three

Let us then consider the three stages of sexual intercourse that normally should blend into each other.

PREPARATION

For the most part, men are in a constant state of sexual readiness, even when it is the farthest thing from their minds. Nature made him the hunter, the aggressor, the protector, and in most cases, the initiator. But Nature also requires that he woo and court his dame and win her over. Even in lower animals the female of the species must be courted.

In human beings, the woman longs for and looks forward to being courted and is so designed that she may require some little time to respond adequately to the wooing of the man. But although this desire in a woman is slow in awakening, once awakened, it is often capable of greater expression. Yes, her ultimate orgasm may be as great or even greater than in the male. A few suggestions seem in order for the young bridegroom, although most of these things have already been mentioned in this booklet along the way.

First of all, caresses must be gentle, never harsh, brusk, or forced. If they are light, fleeting and teasing in nature they serve to arouse the imagination to a much greater degree.

When a caress is too prolonged or too persistent, it runs the risk of becoming boring. Even worse it may become irritating or annoying. The lips, the breasts (especially the nipples) and the clitoris are the principal erotic areas, and skillful stimulation of these usually provoke a crescendic desire for intercourse.

Fifty-four

A groom should not be discouraged if his wife does not respond right away, since fear of being hurt may be foremost in her mind. But generally a gentle stimulation of these areas will produce not only a desire, but almost a demand for more and more stimulation.* One can recognize the readiness of the wife by a copious outpouring of secretion from the vagina.

Usually at this moment the bride will express an overwhelming desire for penetration of the male organ. Further stimulation of the clitoris at this point may produce orgasm in the female without penetration of the penis, which in some women would be as undesirable as 'premature ejaculation" in the male. For this reason stimulation should cease temporarily until insertion is accomplished.

THE SEX ACT PROPER

With the insertion of the penis the sex act proper begins. Assuming the female has previously been prepared, the in-and-out motions of the male organ within the vagina usually produces a rather prompt orgasm in the male that culminates in ejaculation of a quantity of milky fluid called semen. Ideally the female achieves her orgasm at this same moment, coinciding with orgasm or ejaculation in her husband. The female orgasm consist of a series of rapid spasmodic contractions in and around the genital organs along with a blinding, pleasantly overwhelming feeling of ecstasy, a feeling that hopefully is shared concurrently by her husband.

The female organs do not ejaculate as is commonly thought, but the vaginal secretion is greatly increased at the time of orgasm.

Fifty-five

What I have described is the ideal situation, the concomitant climax in both husband and wife. Seldom is this ultimate in timing achieved immediately, or even in the first few months of marriage. However, a few suggestions may help.

Although most sensation of a climax is experienced in the spasmodically contracting vagina, there is also great feeling and sensitivity in the clitoris. The clitoris is a small, elongated, highly sensitive body, usually about three quarters of an inch long, situated at the top of the vulva, just above the urethra. In essence it is a miniature penis without a urinary opening. Composed of erectile tissue, it becomes rigid upon stimulation and if titillated long enough, it will eventuate in a so-called clitoral orgasm.

Normally the clitoris is manually stimulated along with caresses upon the lips and the breasts, hopefully arousing the wife to a pre-climatic state, at which time the male mounts and effects penetration. However, many women find it necessary to continue the stimulation of the clitoris in order to come to a complete climax. In this case, it is advisable for the husband or the wife (some find it easier for the wife to accomplish this) to maintain a titillating finger upon the clitoris even though the husband has penetrated. This is done until climax in the wife is complete and emotional relief has been achieved.

In some cases there is sufficient stimulation of the penis to the vagina or even to the clitoris to bring the wife to a climax. But where this is not the case, it is better to keep a finger (husband's or wife's) upon it, either to press it against the penis or actually to continue to titillate it until climax is achieved and completed. Often this method allows for better timing of the orgasm to correspond with that of her husband.

Too often, if the husband penetrates the vagina too early i.e. before the wife is sufficiently aroused, he will ejaculate too soon, leaving her in an unsatisfied, highly keyed-up, completely frustrated condition. If this occurs, the husband should manually titillate the clitoris while continuing other caresses until his wife has reached her climax and finds welcome relief from the emotional build-up.

Although the most common position is that of the man upon the woman, this is by no means the only proper way, nor is it the most satisfactory position for all couples. To each husband and wife is left the initiative to discover the most satisfying position FOR THEM, and also the variation of the techniques herein described.

Remember, it takes time and effort to develop a synchronous relationship. But continued bungling begets boredom as well as resentment so it behooves every husband to develop the most satisfying relationship possible with his wife.

There are no normals to go by as to frequency of intercourse and this must be determined by each couple for themselves. Averages are given in this booklet, but that is all they are.

If desires in the husband and wife do not coincide, a compromise can usually be found that answers the needs of both. Above all, rejection of either one must be avoided.

Fifty-seven

There is no heartbreak equal to the heartbreak of humiliation. And by contrast there is no greater reward than the appreciation of full acceptance.

A wise woman soon learns that an appreciated husband will lay the world at her feet, but a scorned man will soon withdraw his love and seek companionship elsewhere. If she does not desire intercourse as frequently as he, a wise wife will still find great joy in just being loved and wanted. She can easily feign orgasm or let her husband know that, although she does not climax each time, she thoroughly enjoys being loved by him and bringing him such joy.

AFTERPLAY

After the orgasm both husband and wife feel a certain relaxed serenity. Each has a distinct feeling of satisfaction at having brought great joy to the other. They feel a lovely languor that eventuates in a deep, relaxed, refreshing sleep. However, there are a few precious moments just before they sleep when all is well between them. Never have they felt closer to each other than they do now. Never has their marriage meant more to them than now.

This is the sacred opportunity when a husband can embrace his wife firmly yet tenderly as he reaffirms his love for her and reassures her importance in his life. Generally the expression is mutual. To miss this afterglow is to pass by some of the finest moments of life. To experience them, is to live the fuller life.

Fifty-eight

CHAPTER 12

Control of Conception

Aside from complete abstinence or surgical removal of the organs, there is NO absolutely 100% effective method of birth control or contraception. So-called birth-control pills more than any other, however, approximate this optimum. This, along with other methods and their effectiveness will be discussed in this chapter.

SAFE PERIOD

The method known as the "safe period" or the "rhythm method," is widely used, especially by certain religious groups who do not wish to use artificial methods of birth control. More accurate, however, would be the title, "relatively" safe period, for the average woman's cycle is unpredictable. Many women will occasionally be vulnerable or "unsafe," when they should be safe from conception.

The rhythm method is based upon the assumption that the average woman "ovulates" or gives off an egg from her ovary every 28 days and that this ovulation occurs approximately 14 days before her next expected menstrual period is due to begin. Therefore, the "fertile" time for a 28-day-cycle person is just 14 days before her next expected menstrual period, and in this case, 14 days AFTER her last menstrual period has begun.

On the other hand, if a woman has a 35 day cycle, her fertile time would still be 14 days before her next expected menstrual period, but it now would be 21 days *after* the first day of her last menstrual period. The farther from this fertile time one departs, the "safer" the time becomes.

Hence, in a 28 day-cycle woman, the "safest time" would be just before and just after a menstrual period. Allowing three or four days on either side of the ovulation time as fertile, then any remaining days should be relatively safe.

One method of determining the safe period is to record one's temperature the first thing in the morning(preferably at the same time each day) and watch for the customary rise of four tenths to eight tenths of a degree at the fertile time. This same method may be used to determine the optimum time for conception as well as contraception.

CONDOM OR SHEATH METHOD

The male may use a condom, rubber sheath, or "prophylactic" as it is called, to contain the semen and sperm at intercourse to prevent conception. Such a method is effective and especially adapted to the couple in which the wife is unable or unwilling to use any contraception. Precaution should be taken to check the sheath first to be sure there are no leaks and it should also be placed on the penis BEFORE coitus is begun. Many couples do not realize that the cause of their contraception failure was the fact that some sperm may be lurking in the male urethra and can effect conception WITHOUT ejaculation.

DIAPHRAGM WITH JELLY METHOD

A diaphragm used with jelly or cream is extremely effective and also is harmless as a method of contraception. The diaphragm must be fitted by a physician, but it is practically worthless unless combined with a jelly or contraceptive cream (other than petrolatum).

Generally speaking, a diaphragm cannot be fitted in a virgin because of the tight hymenal ring, but the bride can return to her doctor right after marriage for a fitting. At this time she should be instructed on the correct insertion of the device. Also she must know that the diaphragm should be left in place a minimum of twelve hours after intercourse.

JELLY OR CREAM ALONE

Spermicidal jellies and creams may be used alone without the diaphragm, but their effectiveness is decreased somewhat. Actually it is not so much the diaphragm that prevents the conception, but the spermicidal effect of the jelly or cream. The diaphragm merely insures that the jelly or cream will be held in place. However, many women have used only these jellies and creams alone for many years, and swear by their effectiveness.

Sixty-one

FOAMS

With the advent of new packaging, it was only natural that jellies and creams would also be placed in containers with compressed air. Such a combination is the FOAM that is now so widely used. For the most part, the effectiveness of foam approximates that of jelly or cream alone, but it may be more convenient to use. However, like the diaphragm, jelly, cream or condom, it must be applied BEFORE intercourse begins. Post-coital douching is best delayed until eight to twelve hours after intercourse.

SUPPOSITORIES

These are small pellets of low-melting-point preparations that can be inserted into the vagina prior to coitus. They promptly melt and provide protection equivalent in most cases to that of the jellies, creams and foams.

DOUCHES

The post-coital douche is as old as the contraceptive idea and has been effective for many women. However, it carries a fair risk of pregnancy and should not be relied upon as much as the aforementioned methods. Various preparations of all kinds have been used with testimonials for all. In general, the author cannot recommend these with great assurance.

COITUS INTERRUPTUS

Coitus interruptus or withdrawal has been the commonest method of contraception known to man throughout the ages. In the average man who can judge the exact time of ejaculation, it has proved quite satisfactory and effective. The object is to withdraw the penis from the vagina just prior to ejaculation of the sperm, thus avoiding conception.

Although many husbands and wives find this method satisfactory, there are some disadvantages. First of all, it places a strain upon what otherwise should be an unstrained relationship. Both husband and wife may worry about his withdrawing soon enough. Second, it prevents the husband from completing the act as he normally should. Just at the finest moment of their relationship, he must suddenly withdraw and "interrupt" the embrace.

There is considerable evidence to indicate a damaging psychological effect in some men because of this coitus interruptus. In a sizable number of husbands it is alleged to have caused impotence. It is simply not a healthy or normal way in which to end such an important process. Such an interruption may also prevent the wife from achieving her normal climax since withdrawal comes just as she is beginning or is in the middle of her orgasm.

Lastly, there are often sperm to be found in the normal male urethra that are extruded into the vagina BEFORE ejaculation of the male. These can effect conception, much to the consternation and puzzlement of husband and wife who have tried to be so careful.

INTRAUTERINE DEVICES

Intrauterine devices have been used for many, many years but have been frowned upon by most of the medical profession until the early 1960's. At this time new and safer materials and designs were introduced and the devices came into general favor. The commonest devices used at the present writing are the Lippes Loop, the Hall-Stone ring, the Margulies coil, the Birnberg bow, and the Saf-T-Coil.

These devices are produced in different sizes and with the exception of the steel ring, they are all made of plastic material impregnated with barium sulfate so they will show up on x-ray.

Who should not use an intrauterine device?

1. Those who have an active pelvic infection.

2. Those who have had no pregnancies may have difficulty wearing one because of pain, cramping and the fact that the device is more likely to be expelled in these individuals.

3. Women who have distortion of the uterus by fibroid tumors may not have as much protection with an IUD.

When should the IUD be inserted? Preferably two or three days after the end of a period. Following pregnancy it could be inserted during the first postpartum visit at either four or six weeks.

How long may an IUD be left in place? Indefinitely if there are no complications.

What complications does one have with the IUD? Many women have none.

1. Bleeding. About 15% of the women have sufficient bleeding during the first year to require removal of the device. About 10% more have to be removed during the second year.

2. Expulsion. About 10% of the IUDs are expelled spontaneously during the first year but relatively few in subsequent years. However, a woman whose IUD has been expelled may be able to retain a second IUD that is inserted.

3. Some women have a considerable amount of vaginal discharge due to the IUD and occasionally this is sufficient to warrant removal of the device.

4. Pelvic infections are not common with the device but they do occur sometimes and may be treated with or without removing the device, depending upon the severity.

5. Extra-uterine pregnancy. Ectopic pregnancy may occur with an IUD because the device doese not offer protection against a pregnancy in the tube or the ovary. Although these are less common than without the device, they do still occur.

6. Perforation of the uterus. Rarely, about once in 2,500 insertions of the IUD, is a uterus perforated. However, this is not too serious and is usually recognized by the doctor, but pregnancy may occur if it is not recognized.

MECHANISM OF ACTION

No one is sure how the IUD prevents pregnancy, but most doctors feel that it hastens the passage of the egg through the tube and uterus and thereby decreases the chance of fertilization and implantation.

HOW SAFE IS THE IUD?

Theoretically, the pill is supposed to be almost 100% effective, the IUD is 97.5% effective and the diaphragm and condom about 95% or more. For the woman whose body tolerates the IUD (i.e. does not bleed too heavily or have too much vaginal discharge with its use), it is the ideal contraceptive, for there is nothing the patient has to remember, and its presence is undetectable by either husband or wife.

THE PILL

Perhaps no discovery in medicine of recent years has affected more people and their lives than the contraceptive (and controversial) pill. Even those who have not used it have had much to say about it. Many are the controversies that have arisen and these have not been confined merely to patients. Doctors, clergymen and law-makers have all entered into the foray. The final chapter is far from written, but we can discuss a few facets of this remarkable trouble-preventer or trouble-causer, depending upon our point of view.

The pill is effective as a contraceptive . . . almost 100% effective. Only rarely does a conception occur where it is used faithfully. It is convenient and requires only a good memory. Although it is usually well tolerated, it does have a few disadvantages.

For the most part the pill prevents conception by preventing ovulation. It keeps a woman from giving off an egg, and without an egg, "a hen cannot hatch a chick." However, forgetfulness in taking the daily pill may allow ovulation to take place and herein we have a built-in human hazard.

Ordinarily one day's dose can be missed without ovulation and consequent conception occurring. However, when a pill is forgotten, two pills should be consumed the following day.

The pill, by preventing ovulation, keeps a woman in a "physiological" state of pregnancy and therefore may subject her to any or all of the symptoms that a woman may have during pregnancy. Nausea, fatigue, swelling, weight gain, pigmentation of skin, loss of libido, loss of pleasant disposition, to mention just a few, are some of the symptoms that may occur with the ingestion of the contraceptive pill.

However, many women have *NO* untoward symptoms. And even those who do have such unpleasant symptoms find that if they persist in taking the pill, they overcome all discomfort. Usually any discomfort is more than compensated for by the peace of mind they find in safety from conception.

Birth control pills do not cause cancer. In fact there is some evidence to indicate they may even prevent certain types of cancer.

Do birth control pills cause clots and phlebitis? Yes, there is some evidence to show that they increase the incidence of such clotting slightly more than that of the normal non-pregnant state. However, we should mention that pregnancy increases this risk TWENTY times, yet women do not hesitate to become pregnant. It depends upon the motivation toward contraception.

There is one hazard to birth control pills, however, that is seldom mentioned. In certain women the birth control pill seems to suppress the ovary unduly. In these women, the menstrual period diminishes to a scant flow or even disappears completely. Such women may find difficulty in effecting conception when they discontinue the pill. In other words, they could find themselves relatively less fertile when the desire for contraception is over. This seems to be temporary, however, and the relationship of the pill to reduced fertility *has not been proved.*

Yes, although the final chapter is far from written on the "pill," it will continue to be widely and happily used by many millions of women in the meantime.

CHAPTER 13

Mostly Misconceptions

In this chapter I should like to discuss a few misconceptions and perhaps answer a few questions that arise in the minds of many young people entering this important social transition in life we call marriage. Obviously only a few of many questions can be answered in this limited space.

IS IT HARMFUL TO HAVE INTERCOURSE FREQUENTLY?

The only rule to observe is that it must be mutually agreeable to both husband and wife. There is no physical harm to frequent intercourse. There are many' benefits to intercourse in addition to the bond of love and closeness that it creates in the family. For instance, normal orgasm often acts as a safety valve in relieving emotional tension in either partner. It may well aid in the relief of the nervousness and tension that play such a prominent role in peptic ulcers, ulcerative colitis, high blood pressure and heart attacks.

A thoughtful wife may well sense this need and provide important and life-saving relief from the day's tension in her husband. He, in turn may help her through the tensions of a tedious day by considerate and successful help as she finds relief through orgasm. The same applies when she begins the transition to the menopause.

HOW OFTEN SHOULD NORMAL COUPLES HAVE INTERCOURSE?

This depends entirely upon the couple, their age, health and inclinations. Average for young people in their twenties and thirties would be three or four times per week and tapering off as they become older.

IS THERE ANY HARM IN THE FACT THAT THE WIFE DOES NOT ALWAYS REACH A CLIMAX?

No. It may be that she is tired or for other reasons does not choose to reach a climax. However, because she loves her husband and enjoys being loved, she encourags him to have intercourse, knowing his need for this relationship.

IS IT ABNORMAL IF THE HUSBAND CAN'T WAIT FOR HIS WIFE TO CLIMAX?

It is not uncommon for a man to climax too soon. This is called "premature ejaculation." However, if this is a constant occurrence, it may interfere with normal response on the part of his wife. Several suggestions are in order.

    1. A husband may find he can wait better if he avoids insertion of his penis until his wife is almost ready

for her climax. He can usually bring her to this point by tender, appropriate and fleeting caresses as mentioned earlier in the book.

2. There is an anesthetic ointment the husband can apply to his penis that will numb the nerve endings allowing him to delay his orgasm until his wife is ready. This he can obtain from his physician.

3. If either the husband or wife will continue to titillate the clitoris in the wife AFTER insertion of the penis it will enable the wife to climax *with* her husband. Continued stimulation of the clitoris may be necessary and desirable until she has COMPLETED her climax. If discontinued too soon, it may result in an incomplete climax that leaves the wife tense, unfulfilled and dissatisfied.

IS THERE SUCH A THING AS A FRIGID WOMAN WHO IS INCAPABLE OF CLIMAX?

There may be, but they are extremely rare and usually have some abnormality of their anatomy to account for it. If the wife fails to achieve orgasm after a reasonable length of time, the couple should seek medical counsel.

CAN A WOMAN CONCEIVE EVEN THOUGH SHE DOES NOT HAVE AN ORGASM?

Although some have felt there is a psychological disadvantage, there is no evidence to show that a woman's fertility is greatly diminished if she does not climax. She will still become pregnant.

Seventy-one

SHOULDN'T A WOMAN BE ABLE TO CLIMAX WITHOUT ANY EXTRA STIMULATION?

I don't know if she should, but most women *do not* achieve climax without stimulation of the clitoris and considerable caressing otherwise. This is not to be looked upon as abnormal or unusual. In fact, it is a sin NOT to help the wife achieve her climax by whatever method is necessary.

SHOULDN'T A WIFE HAVE A CERTAIN AMOUNT OF NATURAL DESIRE FOR INTERCOURSE?

Yes, but she may be so tired or even so bored that she has lost interest. Intercourse is and should be a mutual thing. *Both* husband and wife must put forth effort to make it a meaningful part of their marriage, something in which both of them share a part of themselves.